Leandro Renan da Silva Miller

School Physical Education

Leandro Renan da Silva Miller

School Physical Education

Implications for pedagogical practice in Youth and Adult Education (EJA)

ScienciaScripts

Imprint
Any brand names and product names mentioned in this book are subject to trademark, brand or patent protection and are trademarks or registered trademarks of their respective holders. The use of brand names, product names, common names, trade names, product descriptions etc. even without a particular marking in this work is in no way to be construed to mean that such names may be regarded as unrestricted in respect of trademark and brand protection legislation and could thus be used by anyone.

Cover image: www.ingimage.com

This book is a translation from the original published under ISBN 978-3-330-76806-2.

Publisher:
Sciencia Scripts
is a trademark of
Dodo Books Indian Ocean Ltd. and OmniScriptum S.R.L publishing group

120 High Road, East Finchley, London, N2 9ED, United Kingdom
Str. Armeneasca 28/1, office 1, Chisinau MD-2012, Republic of Moldova, Europe
Printed at: see last page
ISBN: 978-620-8-11326-1

Leandro Renan da Silva Miller

School Physical Education: implications for pedagogical practice in Youth and Adult Education.

I dedicate this work to the people who believe in the transformative power of dialogic practice within the educational scene, especially in Youth and Adult Education.

ACKNOWLEDGMENTS

To God for comforting me and giving me the strength to complete this work.

To the teaching staff of this institution for contributing and sharing their knowledge during our training as specialists in Education.

To Professor Carlos Sequeira who, with all his humility and wisdom, contributed immensely to the completion of this work, which is so relevant to my academic training.

SUMMARY

INTRODUCTION

In recent years, the number of school dropouts has fallen and the demand for those who were unable to complete their studies on time to return to school has increased considerably. Among the many factors that could explain this phenomenon, the search for a better position in the job market can be highlighted, since in addition to experience, a specific level of education (primary, secondary or higher) is required. Youth and Adult Education (EJA) plays an important role in preparing these individuals for success in their professional development. It's true to say that an EJA class, whatever the stage, is totally heterogeneous, as there are different types of students: those who have gone back to school because their employer will only promote them to a new position if they have the required training; those who have not studied for a long time and have come back just to have a training course, in a form of self-fulfillment; those who need a training course to take the exam in a particular competition and; finally, those students considered to be undisciplined who, after having failed for several periods, are transferred to the EJA class because they are no longer old enough to study in regular education. Faced with this profile of students, the task of teaching is becoming increasingly challenging, as the educator has to develop pedagogical proposals that can reach all the types of individuals mentioned above.

School Physical Education as a curricular component plays an important role in the educational scenario (which includes the EJA) due to its repertoire of topics that can be discussed, analyzed and clarified in a critical and relevant way between educators and students. The search for meaningful learning for EJA students is a constant challenge for educators, as it involves keeping them focused, raising doubts and questions about certain subjects and, above all, mediating critical and divergent positions among them. One of the main obstacles that EJA educators find in their students is their self-esteem, which falls far short of what is expected of the individual who sets out to learn. Many of them feel incapable of solving situations proposed by the teacher, they feel intellectually insufficient to argue and criticize a given subject, in other words, any kind of self-expression is disregarded by them. The goal and challenge for these students is to achieve a mere certificate, when in fact their main objective should be to build meaningful knowledge that they can share with their peers. Physical education in this segment is met with a certain amount of resistance, as it is unfortunately still seen as a "soccer and fireball class", when in reality it can make a significant contribution to the student's all-round development, including improving their own self-esteem.

Based on this assumption, the following question arises:

Is pedagogical practice a facilitating agent in improving the participation of EJA students in Physical Education classes?

As has already been said, Physical Education has a wide range of themes, which makes it possible to learn in countless ways. It is therefore necessary for the educator, after a diagnostic assessment, to draw up a pedagogical proposal that is coherent with the profile and reality of their students, so as to awaken new thinking and new actions among the students.

The general objective of this study is to identify pedagogical practice as a facilitating agent in improving the participation of EJA students in school physical education classes. To this end, it is based on the following research questions:

- What is the pedagogical proposal for teaching Youth and Adult Education?
- What is the role of Physical Education within the current school context?
- What is pedagogical practice and what role does it play in the construction of the physical education teacher's classroom?

Once the research questions have been defined, the following specific objectives have been established:

- Explain the pedagogical proposal for teaching Youth and Adult Education.
- Discuss the role of Physical Education in the current school context and its role in the EJA.
- To present the relevance of pedagogical practice in the construction of the physical education teacher's classroom.

Based on the assumption that Physical Education, within the school setting, is the discipline that introduces and integrates the individual into the body culture of movement, making it possible to experience and understand the various body manifestations that have been historically accumulated and socially transmitted, and Youth and Adult Education, which is the modality created for those who were unable to complete their studies at the appropriate age, the following hypothesis is raised for this research: dialogic pedagogical practice is a facilitating agent for the participation of YAE students in Physical Education classes.

This study has limitations typical of indirect and bibliographical research and is limited to aspects pertinent to School Physical Education and implications for its pedagogical practice in Youth and Adult Education. The approach used in this study takes place from the perspective of a critical conception of education, based on the Progressive Liberationist and Social Criticism of Content tendencies, based, respectively, on a Freirian perspective of education and on a perspective that considers the school to be a suitable environment for the democratization of education, understanding this tendency as a pedagogical practice centered on a dialogical context.

This study is justified by the researcher's role as a Physical Education teacher in Youth and Adult Education classes, and its relevance is to emphasize that dialogic pedagogical practice is a reference for the Physical Education teacher who works in this segment of education, It is also important to emphasize that dialogic pedagogical practice is a reference for the physical education teacher who works in this segment of education, who can contribute to the construction and reconstruction of these individuals as critical beings, autonomous and aware of their actions, for the full exercise of their citizenship and thus making it clear that the role of physical education classes is not only focused on procedural content, but also centered on conceptual and attitudinal issues.

The methodology chosen for this study was bibliographic analysis, of a qualitative nature. This choice was based on the impossibility of carrying out fieldwork. This research is based on theorists such as Paulo Freire, Suraya Darido, Libaneo, Mizukami, Barbosa, among others, who point to and believe in dialogic pedagogical practice as a relevant tool for student participation and commitment in the construction of knowledge in the classroom. Quality, productive and critical teaching must be the constant quest of an educator who is truly committed to building independent beings in their views on social, political and cultural issues. It is hoped that this theme can be another relevant piece of work in the search for a more qualified education for those who were unable to complete their studies in regular education and that it can serve as a tool for consultation and study for the production of further work involving and discussing the proposals presented here.

For a better understanding of the subjects dealt with here, this monograph has been structured as follows:

- INTRODUCTION: composed of the presentation of the study problem, contextualized with arguments that justify and declare the academic and social importance of the research; the statement of the problem, study questions, general objective and specific objectives; the identification of the methodology used, its limitations and delimitation of the theme, as well as the structural organization.
- DEVELOPMENT: composed of the presentation of the information found during the literature review and the articulation of this information in search of answers to the study questions formulated.
- - FINAL CONSIDERATIONS: consisting of the presentation of the final considerations which aim to provide answers to the research questions presented in the introduction.

CHAPTER I - THE PEDAGOGICAL PROPOSAL FOR TEACHING YOUNG PEOPLE AND ADULTS.

The aim of this chapter will be to explain the pedagogical proposal for teaching in Youth and Adult Education, where it will be pointed out, its objectives and forms of legislation, its relations with the progressive pedagogical tendencies: liberating and critical social content, the teacher and the student of this modality and the EJA curriculum proposal related to the common national base.

Not all individuals are able to complete their studies on time, i.e. within the timeframe stipulated as ideal, which is 08 (eight) years for primary education and 03 (three) years for secondary education, due to numerous factors that interrupt the learning process. In order to promote the return of this population, those responsible for the Brazilian education system introduced the modality that is defined as Youth and Adult Education (EJA), which according to the Law of Guidelines and Bases of National Education (LDB) 9394/96, Article 37, paragraph 1, says it **will be aimed at those who did not have access to or continuity of studies in primary and secondary education at the proper age**.

According to Brasil (2000, p.5) it says:

> Youth and Adult Education (EJA) represents an unrepaired social debt towards those who have not had access to or mastery of writing and reading as social goods, whether at school or not, and who have been the labor force used to build wealth and raise public works. Being deprived of this access is, in fact, the loss of an essential tool for a meaningful presence in contemporary social life.

In fact, the search for this lost time is important, because the acquisition of knowledge, the identification of concepts, the understanding of facts and events, all contribute to the formation of today's active and critical citizen. Taking this issue to the professional side, it means that the slightest lack of information excludes the individual from the competitive system in the search for a prominent position in the job market.

In an attempt to minimize the damage caused by the absence of these individuals in the classroom, different functions have been proposed to establish themselves as parameters and facilitators of the students' development: reparative function, equalizing function and qualifying function.

Thus, Brasil (2000, p.9) comments on the reparative function:

> The restorative function must be seen, at the same time, as a concrete opportunity for young people and adults to attend school and as a viable alternative in view of the socio-cultural specificities of these segments for whom effective action is expected from social policies. This is why the EJA needs to be thought of as a proper pedagogical model in order to create pedagogical situations and meet the learning needs of young people and adults.

It's not just about returning to the school environment, but more than that, it's essential to offer quality teaching and recognize the characteristics of each individual. The school is the place where the right to democracy can be exercised most effectively, as it helps to eliminate discrimination and opens up space for students to express themselves freely.

In relation to the equalizing function, Brasil (2000, p.9) states that:

> The equalizing function of the EJA will cover workers and many other social segments such as housewives, migrants, pensioners and prisoners. The re-entry into the education system of those who have been interrupted by repetition, drop-out, unequal opportunities to remain in school or other adverse conditions, should be welcomed as a corrective, albeit belated, repair of archaic structures, enabling individuals to make new inroads into the world of work, social life, the spheres of aesthetics and the opening up of channels for participation.

Providing individuals, regardless of their origin, with an education where they can build their potential, develop skills, contextualize knowledge acquired outside of school, is of paramount importance for the exercise of citizenship and for their participation as active beings in this society. While recognizing the biological individuality of beings, educators must promote teaching that is always aimed at the joint growth of their students, especially in EJA classes, where the differences are clearer.

In relation to the qualifying function, Brasil (2000, p.11) says:

> This task of enabling everyone to update their knowledge throughout their lives is the permanent function of the EJA, which can be called **qualifying**. More than a function, it is the very meaning of the EJA. It is based on the incomplete nature of the human being, whose potential for development and adaptation can be actualized in school or non-school settings. More than ever, it is a call for permanent education and the creation of a society educated for universalism, solidarity, equality and diversity.

When referring to the nomenclature of Young People and Adults, one arrives at the following reasoning: there is no age limit, that is, at any time of life, one can learn, and this learning is a continuous process, believing that the individual is an unfinished being, within an educational perspective. The production of qualified teaching materials by people who are competent and committed to the EJA will have a significant impact on the development and construction of values within the school environment, with the hope that this will lead to personal fulfillment on the part of the student.

As mentioned above, access to this type of schooling has no restrictions as to maximum age or previous studies. At most, an assessment of knowledge and experience is allowed, which indirectly represents acceptance of the validity of so-called hidden curricula (NISKIER, 1997).

It's worth noting that all that's needed is for the individual to be willing to return to school and, through a diagnostic assessment, to determine their level of knowledge and assign them to a suitable class. Another important factor is that in order to cater for this student profile, their socially and culturally acquired knowledge will be analyzed.

Reinforcing this idea, Niskier (1997, p.196) says:

> The methodology for such cases must take into account the maturity and experience of the student, which requires the attention of specialized teachers, i.e. teachers whose preparation goes beyond the routine curricula of pedagogy faculties.

Once again, the educator plays an important role in the learning process, because through his sensitivity in analyzing the real needs of his students, he promotes a situation where teaching is possible so that this individual can develop in a meaningful way.

Corroborating this analysis, Niskier (1997, p.196) states that:

> Hence the need for a specialized teacher, capable of understanding all these problems and approaching them in a different way to that used with mainstream students. They are two completely different types in terms of their needs and maturity.

It is at this moment that a committed educator makes the difference, as he puts into practice all the knowledge he has acquired, looking for an alternative way of teaching that respects the differences and characteristics of his students, so that there is no favoritism for some and prejudice for others. Each student has his or her own history and peculiarities, which can be put to good use at some point in the teaching process.

The search for a certain pedagogy that satisfies and contributes to the teaching-learning process corresponding to the EJA population is a constant challenge for teachers in this modality.

However, through an analysis of the pedagogical tendencies that have played different roles within the educational scene, two progressive ones stand out: Liberating Pedagogy, which has had a direct influence on Youth and Adult Education, and the Critical-Social Pedagogy of Contexts, which is still influential today, as it allows for a dialogical relationship between teacher and student, which is fundamental for the development of this student profile.

1.1 - Youth and Adult Education and the progressive tendencies: liberation and social criticism of content.

Brazilian education has always been heavily influenced by liberal pedagogical thinking, understood as a manifestation of the interests of capitalism and made up of traditional pedagogy, new pedagogy and technicist pedagogy.

Trying to define this trend, Libaneo (1998, p.116) says:

> Liberal pedagogy is termed "non-critical" because it does not take into account the implications of the socio-structural determinants of education and thus upholds the idea that the school's function is to prepare individuals according to their aptitudes to play the social roles required by class societies.

This tendency meets the requirements of the ruling class, i.e. the rules are pre-established, the teacher and the books become the sole holders of the truth and it is up to the student to simply memorize the information and reproduce it, without even having the possibility of reflecting or arguing. Nowadays, this archaic tendency can be seen in many institutions, which explains the great delay in educational development, especially in public schools.

In opposition to liberal pedagogy, progressive pedagogy includes tendencies that conceive of education as being inserted in the context of social relations, where antagonistic interests between fundamental social classes coexist, thus attributing socio-political purposes to it within a historical-social project of human emancipation (LIBANEO, 1998).

Thus, Libaneo (1998, p.117) says:

> Depending on the training objectives and processes adopted, progressive pedagogy has manifested itself in liberating (inspired by Paulo Freire's pedagogical thinking) and libertarian (inspired by self-management and/or anti-authoritarian proposals) versions, as well as in cultural content pedagogy.

By trying to bring education closer to the context of social relations, this trend gives the individual, in this case the student, the chance to express an opinion, to criticize, to question, in other words, to enter the teaching process as the subject of learning, exercising their right to citizenship and more than that, they build their autonomy in a consistent way, based on their culturally experienced knowledge associated with that acquired through knowledge.

In establishing a parameter between the tendencies, the research will limit itself to presenting below some characteristics of liberating pedagogy and critical social pedagogy of the contents, of a progressive nature, understanding that these two are closer to the teaching proposal in relation to Youth and Adult Education, which is the main intention.

These manifestations of progressive pedagogy do not have a tradition within Brazilian pedagogical thought; nor can it be said that they have generated different school practices in relation to liberal pedagogy. However, it has exerted a marked influence on the actions of educators, intellectuals and political activists interested in educational proposals geared towards a conception of education as an emancipatory activity (LIBANEO, 1998).

In a society where the liberal tendency predominates, the result of a totally capitalist and elitist government, although the current rulers are of socialist origin, the practice and use of the progressive tendency within the educational scene becomes utopian. However, as argued above, there are educators who are gradually introducing and presenting this trend.

Liberating Pedagogy was proposed by Professor Paulo Freire, considered the father of Youth and Adult Education. In this author's work, man is the subject of education, the more he reflects on reality, on his own concrete situation, the more he becomes progressively and gradually aware, committed to intervening in reality in order to change it (MIZUKAMI, 1986).

Therefore Mizukami (1986, p.86-87) says that:

> Since man is the subject of his own education, every educational activity should promote the individual himself and not be an instrument for adjusting him to society. It will be thanks to critical consciousness, the characteristics of which will be analyzed later, that he will increasingly take on this role of subject, choosing and deciding, finally freeing himself.

He goes on to say (1986, p.90):

> Man builds himself up and becomes a subject to the extent that, integrated into his context, he reflects on it and commits himself to it, becoming aware of his historicity. Man is constantly challenged by reality and must respond to each of these challenges in an original way.

Man, therefore, becomes the center of the learning process, and the educator's greatest challenge is to provide alternatives for development, and to mediate reflective support that the subject himself makes around his reality. It is the change of the individual from being passive to active, becoming committed and questioning society.

Liberating pedagogy must seek to overcome the oppressor-oppressed relationship. Overcoming this type of relationship requires conditions in liberating praxis, where dialogue plays a fundamental role in the perception of the oppressor's reality (MIZUKAMI, 1986).

The teacher-student relationship must be horizontal and not imposed. To this end, the teacher will seek conditions so that the student can perceive the contradictions of society and the groups in which they live.

The methodology used in this pedagogy, according to Freire, involves the following phases: a survey of the vocabulary of the groups being worked with; the choice of generating words; the creation of existential situations typical of the groups to be taught literacy; the creation of a script sheet and the preparation of sheets with the breakdown of the phonetic families corresponding to the generating words and a discovery sheet, containing the phonemic families, which is used to discover new words with those syllables (MIZUKAMI, 1986).

This literacy method developed by Freire reflects his approach to education. Although it is closely linked to Youth and Adult Education, in theory this approach sees education as a continuous process and has profound implications for mainstream education.

However, in practice, these positions reflect, on the one hand, the devaluation of formal education and contempt for its teaching functions, in favor of informal, popular, unsystematic education, ignoring the school. This is because this tendency criticizes current education, believing that its function is to reproduce class society and, consequently, the capitalist mode of production (LIBANEO, 1985).

It should be made clear that Paulo Freire created his method and used it in an out-of-school environment, i.e. in an informal context, in the working classes, where the illiteracy rate was high among adults, with the aim of promoting a new way of thinking and acting among these individuals. When it entered the formal environment, i.e. the school environment, Liberating Pedagogy faced great difficulty in being accepted or disseminated, because its proposals conflicted with the educational proposal of the current system, which is the reproduction of classes, of robotic and mechanized beings, while the other proposed that of autonomous and critical beings.

In contrast, the Critical Social Pedagogy of Content values the school as a mediator between the student and the world and fulfills this role through the process of critical transmission/assimilation of knowledge. The dissemination of content is the primary task. Not abstract content, but living, concrete content that is therefore inseparable from social realities (LIBANEO, 1998).

In relation to the school's task, Libaneo (1998, p.39) states that:

> Valuing the school as an instrument for the appropriation of knowledge is the best service that can be rendered to popular interests, since the school can contribute to eliminating social selectivity and making it democratic. If the school is an integral part of society as a whole, acting within it is also acting towards the transformation of society.

In this pedagogy, the school's role is to prepare students for the world and its possible contradictions, providing them with the means to position themselves consciously and critically in the face of these situations, contributing to the formation of a more active and participatory society.

The teaching content in Critical Social Pedagogy consists of universal culture, which is a domain of relatively autonomous knowledge, incorporated by humanity, but constantly reassessed in the light of social realities (LIBANEO, 1998).

When educators accept relatively autonomous knowledge, they take on an important role in this process and provoke in students the possibility of new forms of critical evaluation of this content.

While in Liberating Pedagogy, the teacher-student relationship, knowledge results from the exchanges that are established in the interaction between the environment and the subject, with the teacher being the mediator, in the Critical Social Pedagogy of the Contexts, this relationship, in its pedagogical nature, consists of providing the conditions in which teachers and students can collaborate to make these exchanges progress. The teacher's role is irreplaceable, but the student's participation in the process is also emphasized (LIBANEO, 1998).

The student, with his experience in a cultural context, searches for the truth by comparing it with the content and models presented by the teacher. The educator, who has been trained to teach, has knowledge and it is up to him to analyze the content and compare it with social realities, awakening the student's critical sense.

Regarding teaching methods in this pedagogy, Libaneo (1998, p.40-41) says:

> The methods of a critical social pedagogy of content do not start from artificial knowledge, deposited from outside, nor from spontaneous knowledge, but from a direct relationship with the student's experience, confronting the knowledge brought from outside. The work of the teacher relates the practice of the students to the content proposed by the teacher, at which point there is a "break" from the poorly developed experience. This break is only possible when the teacher explicitly introduces new elements of analysis to be critically applied to the student's practice.

It is clear that the teacher plays a fundamental role in the student's development process by proposing teaching methods that focus on the interaction between content and social realities. It's clear that a well-designed political-pedagogical proposal, tailored to the real needs of a given community, will make a major contribution to the transformation and democratization of that area.

In short, the Critical Social Pedagogy of Contexts proposes the democratization and conscientization of mankind, using the school as the main channel for this process, given that it is in this environment that individuals can exchange ideas and share their cultural reality. The teacher, as the authority in this scenario, leads the debate, intervening and questioning through dialogue and ends up awakening in the student a new way of conceiving a certain subject and, above all, places him or her as a participant and active subject in the process of overcoming submission.

After a brief analysis of Liberating Pedagogy and Critical Social Pedagogy of Contexts, we concluded that their contributions to the development of the individual have been significant, given that both promote a horizontal teacher-student relationship, i.e. there is dialogue, and realities are confronted through certain themes, allowing for various angles of analysis and seeking a new critical view of the individual. Bringing these pedagogies together for teaching in Youth and Adult Education reveals two situations: as has already been said, the liberating pedagogy, although focused on adult education, does not consider formal education, understanding that it is an institution that serves the interests of the ruling class, which would imply that it should be chosen as a teaching model; and the critical social pedagogy of the contents already emphasizes that democratization can only be achieved when culturally experienced knowledge is brought closer to the knowledge that comes from living with the educator, who plays the role of leading this confrontation of realities, through dialogue and questioning, within an appropriate environment, which is the school; this teaching profile is closer to the pedagogical proposal of Youth and Adult Education.

1.2 - The Youth and Adult Education teacher.

In order to achieve acceptable levels of educational quality for the population, it is essential to train qualified and specialized teachers. For this to happen, it is necessary to invest in teaching, both for those preparing to teach and for professionals in the field. These incentives would come through valuing education professionals, continuing education courses, symposiums, lectures, congresses, books, access to information technology such as the Internet, teaching software, among others. This is an issue that needs to be analyzed very carefully.

In light of this, Demo (1999, p.87) warns:

> The issue of teachers is a complex one, including at least two major areas: professional development and technical competence. The problem is one of formal and political quality. Formal quality is due to the fact that primary school teachers do not usually have adequate training. In terms of political quality, the issue is also very serious, because if basic education is the fundamental instrument of citizenship, the teacher cannot be an agent of citizenship without being a citizen himself.

Arguing about the issue of teachers is a complicated task, as it involves questioning various factors that directly influence the development of this professional's work. The purpose of this comment is to shed light on the respect that should be shown to educators, both in terms of salaries and educational development policies.

One of the main tasks of educators is to awaken their students' critical sense. In Youth and Adult Education, this task becomes more arduous, because in certain situations the educator encounters students who are very low in criticality due to their low self-esteem. Stimulating, encouraging, questioning and provoking are great ways of reversing this level of student confidence. The search for student autonomy is an incessant quest for the committed and transforming educator.

According to Libaneo (1998, p.139) in relation to teaching work he says:

> Teaching work, then, consists of the action of the teacher in the educational act (with the support of the school institution as a whole), measuring the processes by which the student appropriates or re-appropriates the knowledge of their culture and that of the dominant culture, rising from common sense to critically elaborated knowledge.

Teaching represents a mediating activity between the individual, in this case the student, and social and historically accumulated culture. The school would be the meeting point of this situation, rejecting the belief that it is merely an apparatus for the reproduction of social classes. In this educational process, teachers need to use didactic means that stimulate student participation, always respecting the cultural differences of each one.

The preparation of a teacher for the EJA must include, in addition to the training requirements for any teacher, those related to the differential complexity of this type of teaching. Thus, this teaching professional must be prepared to interact empathetically with this group of students and to establish dialog (BRASIL, 2000).

This more flexible position of the teacher makes it possible to have a more harmonious relationship with the students, given that most of them are in the same age group as the teacher. The recovery of self-esteem, the search for a social meaning for skills, the appreciation of the knowledge acquired and, above all, the teacher's encouragement are important reasons for the individual who studies in the EJA to remain in school, combating possible possibilities of school dropout. The overcoming of this student is represented by the fact that the teacher, as mediator of the educational process, respects and questions the student's existing knowledge.

Based on this, Freire (1996, p.30) states that:

> Teaching requires respect for the students' knowledge: that's why thinking correctly places a duty on the teacher or, more broadly, the school, not only to respect the knowledge with which the students, especially those from the lower classes, come to it - knowledge socially constructed in community practice - but also, as I've been suggesting for over thirty years, to discuss with the students the raison d'être of some of this knowledge in relation to the teaching of the content.

Discussing concrete reality and associating it with the subject whose content is being taught is of the utmost importance in the student's overcoming process. Establishing a link between the knowledge acquired at school and life experience provokes a transformation in the individual's way of thinking, and the educator needs to take on this role of provocateur and questioner.

Once again, Freire (1996, p.39) warns that:

> That's why the key moment in ongoing teacher training is critical reflection on practice. It is by thinking critically about today's or yesterday's practice that the next practice can be improved. The theoretical discourse itself, which is necessary for critical reflection, must be so concrete that it almost blends in with practice.

What matters in teacher training is not the mechanical repetition of a gesture, but the understanding of the individual as a whole. Knowing that teaching is not about transferring knowledge, but about creating possibilities for the student's own production or construction. For these achievements in the EJA, the training of competent professionals is necessary, and the attraction of these qualified educators can only be made possible when there are adequate structures in the training institutions.

Respecting the diversity of their students, establishing a dialogical relationship, where the teacher is an authority and not an authoritarian, seeking to build authentic and critical beings, is one of the goals to be achieved so that dropout does not occur during the school term. Providing a favorable teaching environment is a constant challenge for EJA teachers.

Freire (1996, p.59-60) puts it this way:

> The teacher who disrespects the student's curiosity, his aesthetic taste, his restlessness, his language, more precisely, his syntax and his prosody; The teacher who ironizes the student, who minimizes him, who tells him to "put himself in his place" at the slightest sign of his legitimate rebellion, as much as the teacher who shirks his duty to propose limits to the student's freedom, who shirks his duty to teach, to be respectfully present to the student's formative experience, transgresses the fundamental ethical principles of our existence.

By mentioning the word ethics in the comment above, Professor Paulo Freire shows that teaching requires respect for the autonomy of the student's being, in other words, it is in this sense that the EJA teacher must act, committing himself and assuming his role as a mediating agent, respecting the autonomy, dignity and identity of the student, and in practice, having consistency when teaching. (FREIRE, 1996).

Teachers should take advantage of the space at school to comment on everyday issues and the reality of their students' lives, provoking a critical sense. And show that, as well as discussing "formal knowledge", issues that involve the knowledge already acquired by their students can be debated in a relevant way.

Finally, EJA educators need to be critically aware of the fact that they are living with and sharing moments with individuals - in this case, students - who dream, who project possibilities for achievement, who have come to find a new way of looking at the world, who have come to learn and exchange experiences with others, and who are looking for a place back in society. Progressive educators, who are committed to an education based on dialogue and the exchange of experiences, respecting the cultural diversity of their students, need to recognize that they are unfinished beings, in other words, that educating is an ongoing process.

1.3 - The Youth and Adult Education student.

In general, the profile of an EJA student is characterized by the objective of recovering knowledge that has been stagnant for some time due to a number of factors. However, it is important to point out that while this student no longer has formal knowledge, characterized by school knowledge, he has acquired ways of thinking, through his experiences, which cannot be forgotten or rejected. The teacher has the task of confronting this knowledge, provoking a more concrete way of acting on a given subject, so that students can build critical opinions.

Accustomed to following orders, EJA students are weak in terms of the practice of thinking and making decisions. This increases the school's responsibility as a space capable of encouraging this ability, which is so fundamental to human beings (BRASIL, 2006).

Based on this, Brasil (2006, p.29) states that:

> This means that the EJA classroom has the responsibility to be marked by activities that involve thinking, to the detriment of those that point to the mere memorization of what is intended to be taught. Commenting on what is being learned, taking a position on what has happened and contributing to their own assessment are situations that will certainly contribute to the growth of these students.

It is important for the EJA teacher to create a climate of trust and friendship that allows everyone to participate in the effort to discover what they are trying to learn. It is worth pointing out that the need to know who your student is, and what their needs are at that moment, also contributes to the success of their learning. Valuing life experiences and sharing memorable situations also strengthens the relationship between educators and students.

When analyzing the question of students' knowledge, Freire (1996, p.31) states that:

> Why not discuss with the students the concrete reality to which the subject whose content is being taught should be associated, the aggressive reality in which violence is constant and people live with each other much more than with life? Why not establish an intimacy between curricular knowledge that is fundamental to students and the social experience they have as individuals?

It is important for students to be aware of their relevant participation in the educational process, and thus assume their role as subjects of learning, enabling teachers to adopt a form of teaching based on dialog, the confrontation of ideas and the exchange of experiences. The students' critical analysis of a given theme or subject enables the teacher to question their thinking, thus stimulating a moment of reflection in which the subject being questioned can be confronted from different perspectives and in different ways. Unifying curricular knowledge with students' social experience is an arduous task, but it is possible, as long as the teacher is committed to his or her role as a transformer.

1.4 - Youth and Adult Education and the common national base of curricular components.

The common national base of curricular components must be included in the EJA. And the students' learning must be such that they are able to continue their studies on a regular basis. The provision of this type of education is therefore subject to primary and secondary education (BRASIL, 2000).

Therefore, Brazil (2000, p.65) states that:

> The national curriculum guidelines for the EJA, as far as primary education is concerned, contain the Common National Base and its Diversified Part, which should be integrated around the curricular paradigm that aims to establish the relationship between Primary Education and Citizen Life, with

> the Areas of Knowledge. As far as secondary education is concerned, the EJA must take into account the knowledge of the curricular areas of Languages and Codes, Natural Sciences and Mathematics, Human Sciences and their respective Technologies.

When the guidelines were defined, Physical Education as a curricular component in both primary and secondary education was given an opportune place in this process, because through the body culture of movement and its themes, it enables a variety of experiences and situations, reaching the three domains of the student's development: cognitive, affective and psychomotor. The next item will investigate the role of this curricular component in the educational scenario, and then present the relevance of its applicability in school physical education classes in the EJA.

CHAPTER II - PHYSICAL EDUCATION IN THE CURRENT SCHOOL CONTEXT AND ITS ROLE IN THE EDUCATION OF YOUNG PEOPLE AND ADULTS.

This chapter investigates the role of Physical Education in the current school context, presenting its concept, identifying the approaches that have influenced its affirmation as a curricular subject, arguing its purpose according to the Education Guidelines and Bases Law, and culminating with its role in Youth and Adult Education.

2.1 - Concept of School Physical Education.

Many studies report the influence of bodily movement in the evolutionary process of human history, be it for reasons of survival by primitive man, for reasons of war preparation as the Romans used it, for reasons of the cult of the body and the unification of peoples as the Greeks believed, up to the present day with the question of the benefits of practicing physical activity as a synonym for a healthier and longer life.

It is possible to perceive the importance that movement has had at certain historical moments and the different reasons for its use and manifestation. Physical Education is therefore understood as the body culture of movement (BRASIL, 1998).

According to Brasil (1998, p.29) school physical education is understood as:

> A subject that introduces and integrates the student into the body culture of movement, forming the citizen who will produce and transform it, equipping them to make use of games, wrestling, sports, dances and gymnastics for the benefit of the critical exercise of citizenship and the improvement of quality of life.

The importance of Physical Education in the school setting is present in the comment above, as it proposes education through movement and not education of movement. It points to the individual as a being who thinks, feels, moves and relates to others, and not one who reproduces movements without knowing their purpose. It is important to comment on the possibilities of teaching through the different bodily manifestations classified under the themes: games, wrestling, sports, dances and gymnastics.

It is therefore up to School Physical Education to give all students the opportunity to develop their potential, in a democratic and non-selective way, with the aim of improving them as human beings (BRASIL, 1998).

After a brief analysis of the concept of School Physical Education, and the current moment that Brazilian education is going through, it indicates that this discipline has a relevant role in the integral development of the individual, because in a society where the issue of competitiveness is increasingly fierce, proposing democratization using movement as a starting point within the school space, reflects as a concrete possibility that everyone has the right to develop their potential within their possibilities.

2.2 - Some pedagogical trends in school physical education.

Some reports say that Physical Education was introduced in schools in Brazil in 1851, with the Couto Ferraz reform. In a reform carried out by Rui Barbosa in 1822, there was a recommendation that gymnastics should be compulsory for both sexes and that it should be offered in normal schools (BETTI, 1991).

It's important to note that Physical Education at this time suffered from a certain prejudice, as the ruling elite associated the practice of physical activity with physical exertion, which in that historical period was the service of slaves.

It was only in the 1920s that several states began to carry out their educational reforms and included Physical Education under the more frequent name of gymnastics. It was included in the law, but it took a long time for the law to be enforced (BETTI, 1991).

Some trends greatly influenced the practice of Physical Education at school in the 20th century, such as the hygienist model, which was aimed at hygiene and health habits; and the militarist model, which was aimed at forming a generation capable of withstanding combat and acting in war. These models didn't require knowledge of the body, but rather being a former practitioner.

Other trends that have influenced and are still present today are the sportivist trend, which emerged at a historical moment in both political and educational history. In the first, the country was under a military regime, in which the school was a major promoter of this system, and in the second, the issue of traditional technical pedagogy had a major influence on the application of sport in schools. The aim of this trend was to train athletes in the quest for a competitive country in sporting events. The other is the recreationist trend, which was applied in a non-directive way and the teacher's role was to offer the ball and set the time.

With the emergence and innovative proposals of progressive pedagogies, the issue of the development of teaching in schools has been the subject of much debate and discussion about its applicability.

As for Physical Education at school, since the mid-1980s there have been changes in its conceptions, in a process that involves various transformations, both in academic research in this segment and in the pedagogical practice of teachers of this curricular component (DARIDO, 2003).

Resistance to the biological conception of Physical Education led to criticism of the predominance of sports content. Thus, in opposition to the more technicist, sportivist and biologist approach, new movements emerged in school Physical Education.

These new trends according to (Darido and Rangel, 2005 p.06) are:

> Humanist, Phemonological, Psychomotricity, based on Cooperative Games, Cultural, Developmental, Interactionist-Constructivist, Critical Overcoming, Systemic, Critical Emancipatory, Renewed Health, based on the National Curriculum Parameters (PCNs/Brazil, 1998), as well as others.

Having stated the trends in school Physical Education, the development of this study will be based on the National Curriculum Parameters document, believing that its proposal is directly involved with the issue of citizenship and thus uses the Body Culture of Movement as a means of intervention to achieve an autonomous and active individual.

2.3 - Physical Education and the National Curriculum Parameters.

Knowing that in a country where the diversity of cultures, income distribution and political issues have a direct influence on its development, there is a proposal for a document that values and respects differences involving the school, teachers, political powers, the community and the students who are the targets to be achieved.

The National Curriculum Parameters were created.

Brito apud Darido and Rangel (2005 p. 17) states that:

> The National Education Council focuses on the PCNs as: a curricular proposal among others, a significant proposal, although not compulsory, and an alternative to the curricular proposals of the states and municipalities.

Even though it is a document produced by the Ministry of Education with the participation of several renowned authors within the educational sphere, its applicability is optional, but it is an instrument of great value in the process of building a full and critical citizen.

Since Physical Education is a subject within the school environment, the construction of a document that contemplates its role in the integral development of the individual was relevant.

Brazil (1998 p.15) states that:

> The National Curriculum Parameters for Physical Education put forward a proposal that seeks to democratize, humanize and diversify the pedagogical practice of the area, seeking to broaden it from a purely biological vision to one that incorporates the student's cognitive, affective and socio-cultural dimensions. It incorporates, in an organized way, the main issues that teachers should consider when developing their work, supporting discussions, planning and evaluations of educational practices.

The presentation of this document makes it clear that it is concerned with seeing the individual who takes part in Physical Education classes at school as a being who is integrated in all aspects and not just indoctrinated into performing movement. This dualistic view can still be found in schools today. Educators need to raise awareness in the search for a full citizen who knows, respects and questions what happens around them.

The National Curriculum Parameters for the area of school Physical Education contribute to the reflection and discussion of pedagogical practice with three fundamental aspects (BRASIL, 1998).

The first aspect, according to Brasil (1998, p.19) is:

> The principle of inclusion, characterized by the systematization of objectives, content, teaching and learning processes and evaluation, aims to include students in the body culture of movement. It seeks to reverse the historical situation in the area of selecting fit and unfit individuals for bodily practices, resulting from the exacerbated valorization of performance and efficiency.

The possibility of experimenting without the responsibility of executing the perfect movement makes it easier for the individual to access Physical Education classes, because the fear of making a mistake ends up intimidating them and consequently they refuse to try, Now, when it comes to improving movement, it's not up to the school or the Physical Education teacher to do this (it's understood that sports clubs have professionals who are paid to do this), but rather to challenge the student to try out new possibilities and thus integrate them into the lessons.

In the second aspect, Brasil (1998, p. 19) talks about:

> The principle of diversity applies to the construction of teaching and learning processes and guides the choice of objectives and content, with the aim of broadening the relationships between the knowledge of the body culture of movement and the subjects of learning. It seeks to legitimize the diverse learning possibilities that are established by considering the students' affective, cognitive, motor and socio-cultural dimensions.

Reaffirming once again that the Physical Education class is not restricted only to the motor aspect, but also to the cognitive, affective and sociocultural aspects, requiring the teacher to take a broader view of his student, analyzing and evaluating in these dimensions, that is, as a whole.

And finally, the third aspect, Brazil (1998, p.19) points out:

> The category of contents, where they are presented according to their conceptual category (facts, concepts and principles), procedural category (linked to doing) and attitudinal category (norms, values and attitudes). Conceptual and procedural content are very close to each other, as the central object of body culture revolves around doing, understanding and feeling with the body. These categories include the learning, organization and assessment processes themselves. The attitudinal contents are presented as objects of teaching and learning, and point to the need for students to experience them in a concrete way in everyday school life, seeking to minimize the construction of values and attitudes through the "hidden curriculum".

The presentation of these categories of content indicates the possibility of the Physical Education teacher's pedagogical practice during their lessons. The different cultural manifestations produced by the individual from the dawn of humanity to the present day, clarified from a conceptual, attitudinal and procedural point of view, will be relevant to the understanding of some behaviors and the use of some body practices.

The National Curriculum Parameters make mention of the issue of Physical Education classes in Youth and Adult Education (EJA) in which they propose the selection of content and the distribution of activities developed according to the characteristics of the course and the group. This diagnostic approach is important for the success of the class, because as was mentioned in Chapter II, the population of the EJA is diverse, so it is necessary to propose something that does not devalue the characteristics and knowledge of each individual.

2.4 - Physical Education and the National Education Guidelines and Bases Law.

As mentioned earlier, Law 9394/96 establishes the guidelines and bases of national education, and in article 26, it states that the curricula of primary and secondary education must have a common national basis, to be complemented by a diversified part, required by the regional and local characteristics of society, culture, economy and clientele.

Therefore, in article 26, paragraph 3, of the Law of Guidelines and Bases 9394/96, Physical Education must be offered as part of the curriculum:

> Integrated into the school's pedagogical proposal, it is a compulsory curricular component of basic education, and its practice is optional for the student:
> I - who works six hours or more;
> II - over thirty;
> III - who is doing initial military service or in a similar situation is obliged to do physical education;
> IV - if they are covered by Decree-Law No. 1,044 of October 21, 1969;
> V - who has offspring.

Even though it is included as a curricular component, it is notable that there are some restrictions that at least raise certain questions about its pedagogical practice in schools. A certain biologist vision of the document's authors stands out in relation to the practice of Physical Education at school, as it exempts all individuals from the aforementioned situation.

In agreement with Darido and Rangel (2005, p. 56):

> Once again, it is also clear how important it is for school PE teachers to convince people in these conditions to take part in their classes, through interesting teaching strategies and by explaining the benefits of practicing.

Convince and present a Physical Education that is not only focused on the execution of movement, but through this manifestation the concepts and procedures are understood, and the attitudes that originate through it are discussed.

2.5 - The inclusion of Physical Education in Youth and Adult Education.

The inclusion of Physical Education in Youth and Adult Education represents the possibility for students to have contact with the body culture of movement. Access to this universe of information, experiences and values is understood as a citizen's right, a perspective for building and enjoying tools to promote health, creatively use leisure time and express affections and feelings in various contexts of coexistence (BRASIL, 2002).

The curriculum proposal for Physical Education in Youth and Adult Education is based on the ideas consolidated by the National Curriculum Parameters and discussed by various authors engaged in the dissemination and massification of the subject in this modality.

According to Brasil (2002 p. 195):

> Developing a Physical Education proposal for Youth and Adult Education is both a necessity and a challenge. It is necessary to recognize that the time has come to look at this segment of Brazilian society and seek new ways of enabling their access to this knowledge.

Providing knowledge using the body culture of movement, providing opportunities for different forms of learning and presenting a new way of thinking about movement are goals to be achieved in Youth and Adult Education. As well as rescuing a group that has been left out of basic education, it is necessary to present Physical Education as a relevant discipline in their integral development as individuals participating in contemporary society.

When it comes to lesson planning, the experience of students in Youth and Adult Education in relation to Physical Education classes should be taken into account.

Brazil (2002, 195) comments on this:

> EJA students already have a representation of the school, physical activity and school physical education, formed from the experiences that make up their personal history; that's why it's important to include in the teaching perspective, as one of the guiding axes of educational actions for young people and adults, the possibility of rescuing the memories built up from different practices.

Valuing and respecting an individual's history is a way of bringing them back to social life in the school environment, from which they were excluded for some reason. Having pointed out the concept of school Physical Education, its different approaches and its role in the Education of Young People and Adults, it is important to point out what pedagogical practice is and its participation in the construction of the Physical Education teacher's classroom.

III - THE RELEVANCE OF PEDAGOGICAL PRACTICE IN THE CONSTRUCTION OF THE PHYSICAL EDUCATION TEACHER'S CLASSROOM.

The aim of this chapter is to present the importance of pedagogical practice in the construction of the physical education teacher's classroom. Having already explained the pedagogical proposal for teaching Youth and Adult Education (EJA) and discussed the role of Physical Education in the current school context and its role within this modality in the previous chapters, we now propose a pedagogical practice that is significant for the integral development of the individual during Physical Education classes.

According to Brasil (2002, p.198), **the pedagogical practice of Physical Education is based on four fundamental aspects: the principle of inclusion, diversity, content categories and transversal themes.**

The aim here is to understand the actions of physical education teachers in a context geared towards participatory planning. When drawing up their teaching plan, the teacher must be familiar with the school's political-pedagogical project, so that this plan is coherent with the students' reality, respecting their characteristics and valuing the knowledge accumulated during each student's career. This is why the participation of the Physical Education teacher in drawing up the school's political-pedagogical project is becoming increasingly necessary. And, what's more, through their knowledge, they can argue and present their discipline as a relevant factor in transforming that particular reality.

According to Veiga *apud* Darido and Rangel (2005, p. 60):

> The political-pedagogical project has to do with the organization of

> pedagogical work on two levels: the organization of the school as a whole and the organization of the classroom, including its relationship with the immediate social context, trying to preserve the vision of totality. On this journey, it will be important to stress that the political-pedagogical project seeks to organize pedagogical work as a whole.

Darido and Rangel (2005, p. 60) further state that:

> Assuming the school organization of curricular components based on a political-pedagogical project and recovering teaching work in the classroom, with a view to building a pedagogical practice centred on student participation, with actions designed for students and, if possible, with them.

Drawing up a political-pedagogical project in which each curricular component is taken into account in accordance with its own characteristics is important if teachers are to work efficiently in their classes. It is true to say that success will only be achieved when all parties are committed to change: the school, teachers, students and the community.

3. 1 - Teaching Physical Education in Youth and Adult Education (EJA).

The issue of teaching Physical Education at school has generated debate, discussion and criticism. Authors propose teaching methodologies based on conceptions they believe are more relevant to the development of the individual. As the proposal of this work is Physical Education in the EJA, the question of what to teach will be focused on the proposal of the National Curriculum Parameters classified as a citizen approach according to Darido and Rangel (2005).

Since the Youth and Adult population is mostly made up of workers and people in the older age groups, proposing a Physical Education class focused on developing physical fitness would be disastrous and would lead to a considerable dropout rate. This is justified by the fact that some studies have shown that practicing activity less than two days a week does not provide any improvement and, in the case of Physical Education classes in the EJA, this time is reduced to a maximum of 1 hour and 30 minutes a week.

Reinforcing this comment, Dantas *apud* Barbosa (2001 p.30) says that **training less than two days a week does not produce adequate changes in either anaerobic or aerobic capacity, or in body composition.**

It's worth pointing out that physical education teachers who use this methodology produce very little for the development of their class, limiting themselves to practicing the activities. The practical part is relevant as long as the content is applied in a way that makes the student think about the purpose of a particular movement and its relevance within the context in which it is situated.

By proposing a class that focuses on the issue of leisure, the teacher is also mischaracterizing his or her pedagogical practice by limiting himself or herself to using the time for recreation, going completely against the grain of the school's principles, which is the construction of an active, critical, questioning and transforming individual. On the other hand, from a recreationalist perspective, the aim is to occupy the individual's time with "fun", giving the illusion that everyone has the same rights.

For further clarification, Dumazedier *apud* Cavalcanti (1984, p.62) defines leisure as **a set of occupations which the individual can indulge in of their own free will, whether to rest, have fun, recreate or entertain themselves**. It is a fact that many Physical Education teachers teach their classes in the aforementioned way these days.

Reinforcing this comment, Cavalcanti *apud* Barbosa (2001, p.29) talks about the definition of leisure:

> This definition of leisure put forward by Dumazedier, and so widely accepted by Physical Education teachers, is formulated "in an abstract framework of needs, as if the man of industrial society were free from social determinisms and could exercise his autonomy in his free time".

This question is easy to observe when the teacher asks the students what the purpose of Physical Education is, and most of the answers say "it's a way of distracting the mind, and it helps to forget the problems of everyday life".

A pedagogical practice committed to the full development of the individual during Physical Education classes has to be based on conceptual, procedural and attitudinal issues, as proposed by the National Curriculum Parameters.

In view of this, Brasil (2002 p.200-201) comments on the content:

> The *procedural* dimension is not restricted to the universe of motor skills, physical abilities and sports fundamentals, but should also include organization, systematization of information and improvement, among others.
> In addition to the *conceptual* content of rules, tactics and some factual historical data on sports, there are also reflections on the concepts of ethics, aesthetics, performance, satisfaction, efficiency, etc.
> Finally, the *attitudinal* content is explained as objects of teaching and learning and is proposed as concrete experiences for the student, which makes it possible to build a position of responsibility towards oneself and others.

Having established the purpose of each dimension, we will now analyze the possibilities for pedagogical practice during Physical Education classes within the themes of Body Culture of Movement, which are: sport, games, wrestling, dances and gymnastics.

It should be made clear that the part that refers to knowledge about the body has not been neglected, but it is understood that the development of the aforementioned themes during Physical Education classes already directly involves it as content to be worked on.

The possibility of working with knowledge about the body in the EJA is interesting and requires teachers to make the most of the time they have during their lessons, since in most schools they are limited to two consecutive lessons of 45 minutes each per week. It is at this point that valuing the students' previous knowledge becomes important for building a meaningful lesson.

3.2 - The pedagogical practice of Sport in Physical Education classes in the EJA.

The issue of sport in Physical Education classes is quite controversial, because even with the proposals of an education where everyone has the right to experience various possibilities, the issue of high performance and the selection of the fittest are still burning within the school scene. In addition to this situation, there is also the rise of sport on the world economic stage, which has become a gold mine for big companies and sports agents. This is why it is so necessary to work on sport beyond motor issues.

According to Brasil (2002, p. 209) on sport:

> Practices that adopt official and competitive rules, organized by regional, national and international federations that regulate amateur and professional play, are considered to be sports. They involve the use of venues - such as fields, swimming pools, tracks, rinks, gyms, etc. - and sophisticated equipment. Media coverage favors their appreciation by a diverse group of social and cultural contingents. For example, the Olympic games, the soccer world cup and certain boxing matches are watched and discussed by a large number of fans and enthusiasts.

The above definition makes it clear that teachers who limit themselves to teaching only the techniques and fundamentals of sport deny their students knowledge that could be relevant to their daily lives, enabling them to understand certain situations involving this world.

Before presenting the conceptual, procedural and attitudinal content, a classification of sport will be presented based on the study by Tubino (2001). This author presents sport in terms of three aspects of its manifestation: educational sport; participation sport and performance sport, although in reality it is not always easy to locate or differentiate between these manifestations (DARIDO E RANGEL, 2005).

Sport in Physical Education classes should be analyzed from three perspectives: regulated sport, sport as something to be learned and sport as something to be watched.

According to Darido and Rangel (2005, p.185), in conceptual terms, regulated sport can be defined as follows:

> To identify the existence of the sports movement as an institutionalized social action that has its specificities, including being regulated by federations, confederations, having a hierarchical structure, organized into different modalities and having its existence independent of the school reality.

Making it possible to discuss what sport is, how certain disciplines came about and through what circumstances, the development of rules (is it fair for everyone?), the question of the positions held and the great interest in being in charge of the functions and the interference of sport in the school is relevant in clarifying some of the questions surrounding this institution.

From a procedural point of view, sport as something to be learned can be worked on as follows, according to Darido and Rangel (2005, p. 185):

> These include the various possible strategies for practicing the sport itself. At this point, students should be encouraged to learn and improve the motor gestures related to the chosen sport, as well as the basics of the tactical strategies needed for the experience.

Introducing the fundamentals of a particular sport as well as the tactical possibilities are important for students' understanding of the sport and the application of certain rules. This is exactly when the issue of selectivity occurs in Physical Education classes, between the most and least able. It needs to be made clear to the student that their motor gesture, as long as it doesn't put their physical integrity at risk, isn't wrong; however, it is considered to be a gesture that doesn't meet the standards required of the high level of a given sport and that is acceptable within their possibilities and experiences.

According to Darido and Rangel (2005, p.187), the attitudinal dimension of sport as something you watch should be argued as follows:

> What is your attitude as a consumer of spectacles and of the universe that surrounds the dissemination and broadcasting of the sporting phenomenon? Two lines can be constructed for work in this dimension: one concerns the unveiling and interpretation of the values and intentions of the media in their broadcasts and the other relates to the position the student assumes in relation to the broadcasts, whether as a mere passive consumer or as an individual who filters and selects the messages, thus constructing a critical and active stance in relation to sport.

Knowing how to be and how to live with issues related to sport is fundamental to understanding how this phenomenon interferes in an individual's day-to-day life. Examples to be mentioned are the World Cup and the Olympic Games, which during their events change the routine of the inhabitants of certain countries around the world, and the fanaticism of clubs, which affects the emotional structure of their fans, who are capable of killing or dying for the honor of their team.

Having presented the possibilities of working with different visions of sport, it is clear that limiting oneself only to teaching the fundamentals and techniques of sport will lead to a great loss in the unveiling of this theme within the school environment. This is why it is necessary for EJA Physical

Education teachers to be aware that the school is not the right place to train sports athletes (even more so in this type of education), but rather to build critical citizens capable of analyzing and questioning issues related to sport.

3. 3 - The pedagogical practice of Games in Physical Education classes in the EJA.

Since ancient times, human beings have played games with each other. A few recorded these games on cave walls in the form of drawings. This and other evidence shows that play has not only accompanied historical evolution, but has also been present in all civilizations. You can find games from Egypt, Greece, India, China, the Incas, Angola, Spain and, of course, Brazil. For example, hopscotch, flying kites or playing pebbles have been recorded in Greece and the Orient, proving the universality of children's games (KISHIMOTO *apud* DARIDO and RANGEL, 2005).

Since the game is a theme of Body Culture, it is possible to understand its importance as a historical and social heritage, practiced and passed down from generation to generation in different ways and possibilities.

Brazil (2002, p.209-210) defines them as:

> Games can be more flexible in their regulations, which are adapted according to the space and material available and the number of participants, among other things. They are played competitively, cooperatively or recreationally in festive, commemorative or socializing situations, or even in everyday life as a simple pastime and diversion. Games include regional games, parlor games, table games, board games, street games and children's games in general.

The use of games in Physical Education classes is important because of their flexibility in the way they work, allowing everyone to participate within their limitations and abilities and providing a satisfying learning moment for the group, as well as a moment of exchange, due to the great diversity that exists, especially in EJA classes.

The ease with which the game can be used as content in Physical Education classes is obvious, as everyone stipulates how it will be played.

Agreeing with this statement, Darido and Rangel (2005, p. 158) present different reasons for the ease with which games can be applied:

> - are not unfamiliar to children, since most of them have already taken part in different games;
> - do not require space or sophisticated equipment (although there may be games with such requirements);
> - can vary in the complexity of the rules, i.e. from a young age you can play games with few rules or games with very complex rules;
> - can be practiced by any age group;
> - are fun and enjoyable for their participants (unless they go to extremes of competition);
> - you learn the game through the global method, unlike sport, which is usually learned/taught in parts. On the other hand, in a great game, you learn by playing, you don't explain and "train" the parts and then play; the fun of learning the game is in actually playing it. You don't learn to throw to then learn to play burnout, you learn to throw during the game. Whether the throw should be stronger, weaker, in a certain direction, up or down, is determined by the context of the game. Collective games were created in this way, people learned by playing, and it was only later, with technique and science, that the decomposition of parts was taught.

In other words, everyone can take part in the game to the best of their ability, regardless of age, as long as everyone's level of demand is respected. Paying attention to the issue of competitiveness during the game is also important if the lesson is to be meaningful for the student. Working on games using alternative materials provides a more comprehensive view of recycling and environmental preservation issues, as well as encouraging students' creativity when making the elements to be used. That's why it's important to use these games during physical education classes in the EJA.

When working with the game in a conceptual dimension, Darido and Rangel (2005, p.160-163) propose the following objectives:

> Get to know the repertoire of games played by family members of different generations and understand the dynamics of the production of games in culture. Distinguish between the characteristics of sports and games, specifically knowing the different ways of organizing space, material resources, rules and forms of organization according to the needs of the group. Knowing the variations in games and play. Understand play from the perspective of leisure and quality of life. Understand the relationship between competitive and cooperative play.

The possibility of understanding the game in a new light from various angles shows how relevant this theme of body culture is during Physical Education lessons at school. Learning about games in different versions, comparing them to sports and pointing out their characteristics, understanding how the game can be flexible to meet the needs of each participant, raising awareness of the practice of games in leisure time as a possibility for quality of life and the differences between competitive and cooperative games are some of the ways of legitimizing the theme of games as an important source of learning.

On a procedural level, Darido and Rangel (2005, p.160) present possibilities for teaching **games** that **can be reproduced, transformed and/or modified in all known ways, as well as carrying out research in the community on the different ways of playing the same game.**

Experiencing variations of certain games helps us understand the diversity of ideas that revolve around a society. Burning, for example, which is played in one way in Rio de Janeiro, is played differently in Amazonas. Bringing these variations closer together enables new ways of practicing a given activity. By getting to know new movements, the individual gains a greater knowledge of their body, building autonomy in the execution of movements during the game.

From an attitudinal point of view, Darido and Rangel (2005, p. 160) propose playing with the questions:

> Linked to values, norms and attitudes, the following can be experienced and discussed, among others: cooperation, solidarity, inclusion, gender relations, ethics, cultural plurality and conflict resolution. The latter dimension, although present in lessons, almost always takes place without the teacher's intervention. Raising the possibility of using it as a lesson objective can be considered an important point in the teacher's work.

This dimension is especially relevant in EJA Physical Education classes, because the great diversity of students, often from very different regions, as well as cultural and religious issues, means that mutual respect, cooperation, inclusion, cultural plurality and conflict resolution take place during the practice of the game, providing a way to accept that differences exist and that they are in everyone's reality.

The game can be considered a valuable tool during Physical Education lessons, provided that the teacher is really aware of this theme in their students' daily lives. It is worth remembering that some studies of human development theory have used play as a basis for reactions to certain stimuli, which to this day serves as a reference for many scholars in the fields of Education and Psychology.

3.4 - The pedagogical practice of Danpas in EJA physical education classes.

It's not uncommon to hear people say that Brazil is the country of dances or a dancing country. This reputation of "ours" is quite pertinent, if we take into account the diversity of rhythmic and expressive manifestations that exist from north to south. Not to mention the immense international repercussions of some of them, such as Carnival (DARIDO E RANGEL, 2005).

Dance is a symbolic representation that has existed since the dawn of humanity and, like writing, emerged as a means of communication and expression between peoples, manifested by various kinds of feelings, such as joy when someone was welcomed by a people, sadness when someone died, and also as a way of revering certain deities in different religious entities.

Corroborating the above comment Darido and Rangel (2005, p. 200) say that:

> In every era and geographical space, dance has been a representation of peoples' manifestations, their "states of mind", their emotions, the expression and communication of their cultural characteristics. Through gestures and movements, dance translates the most intimate of emotions, whether or not it is accompanied by music and singing or by specific rhythms.

Darido and Rangel *apud* Nanni (2005, p. 200) point out that **human beings have used dance as a body language, symbolizing joy, sadness, life and death, to celebrate love, war and peace, in other words, it has represented various aspects of human life**.

Since dance is a rhythmic and expressive activity, it is therefore considered a form of body language, coated with meaning and intentions. They can be performed in a variety of styles and with a variety of rhythms and steps. These include folk dances, ethnic dances, ballroom dances and theatrical dances. As with all the themes of Body Movement Culture, dance has also been the target of social influences, with the practice of classical ballet, for example, becoming the status of nobility for the wealthier classes during the late 19th and early 20th centuries.

Other styles of dance such as rap and funk emerged with the intention of presenting the social ills of a particular group and as a form of protest for a fairer and more humane society.

Dance can have different objectives depending on its context. Darido and Rangel (2005, p.201) propose the following objectives during its development in school physical education classes:

- enable the exploration of creativity through the discovery and search for new forms of body movement;
- making rhythmic education possible by diversifying the dynamics of motor support and by using music, percussion, singing and other resources as instruments to increase motivation;
- to channel expressiveness by reflecting feelings, thoughts and emotions;
- expand your vocabulary and sense of perception;
- broadening horizons and forming critical thinking, leading to participation, understanding, enjoyment and reconstruction of the current conjuncture of the arts and also of the conditions of citizenship;
- lead to artistic appreciation and valorization, emphasizing the cultural and historical contributions contained in dance works.

Dance is a very rich element for Physical Education classes in the EJA, as it allows for the confrontation of ideas and thoughts on certain rhythms and styles, bearing in mind that the main characteristic of the population of this modality is cultural diversity, just as in the game each region has its own way of playing, in dance each person has their own way of expressing themselves and a peculiar meaning for a given rhythmic representation.

As well as dance, manifestations such as mimics, singing toys and cirandas are extremely rich elements for communicating through body expression. These rhythmic and expressive activities provide further support to enrich the process of forming body codes for individual and group communication (BRASIL, 2002).

In relation to dance-related content, there are some qualities of expressive movements. These are: form, space and time, together with the energy expended to carry out the movements. According to Darido and

Rangel (2005, p.202), **knowing the abilities, capacities and possibilities of the body combined with the choreological aspects/ qualities of movement is essential for students to discover how to communicate through dance using their own bodies.**

Offering ways of getting to know their own bodies through dance, mimicry, singing toys or cirandas, helps students to understand the qualities of expressive movements, as well as their duration, intensity and direction.

In a conceptual sense, Darido and Rangel (2005, p.205) say that dance should be worked on in the following way to make it possible:

- Learn about the various manifestations of culture, in different contexts, at different times (ritual, sacred, commemorative, circular dances, etc.)
- Cultivating the Body Culture of Movement through popular culture.
- Discuss the issue of gender and problematize the idea that men don't dance.
- Encourage the habit of reading newspapers and magazines, in which you can see reviews of dance shows, as well as advertisements for performances and their implications, such as ticket prices.
- The issue of inclusion can be addressed in dance classes under well-directed encouragement from the teacher, to make it clear that there is no right or wrong way to dance. Everyone can dance, regardless of biotype, ethnicity or ability.
- Discussing the dangers exposed by the media can be an important way of forming a critical sense.

Through the possibilities presented, working with dance in the EJA in a conceptual dimension will be relevant, because debating the issue of sexism that surrounds this theme, where some men label that this rhythmic manifestation can only be practiced by women, will be relevant to clarifying various questions that involve this subject. Another relevant moment is the question of whether dangar is right or wrong, as many people refuse to dangar on the grounds that they don't know. It is known that there is no instrument for assessing whether a choreography is correct or incorrect. In dance festivals, there are degrees of demand for compliance with certain requirements, which are communicated in advance to the participants, who are fully aware of the demands.

From a procedural point of view, Darido and Rangel (2005, p.206) propose the following way of dancing at school:

- Use techniques and the freedom of spontaneous gestures.
- Use strategies to perceive individual and group rhythms.
- Exploring the development of a sense of space/time/form, in relation to oneself and others, combined with musical stimulation or silence.
- Apply the basic principles of movement qualities or choreological structures to construct choreographic designs.
- Exploration of gestures and codes (techniques) from other body movements or methodological lines of dance styles.
- Understanding the expressive process from individual to collective meanings (mimes, group representations of everyday scenes, individual dangas, small group choreographic drawings, etc.).
- Stimulate the perception of individual and partner body limits through the experience of fluid and elongated movements, creating the opportunity to transcend limitations.
- Experience folk and regional dances by analyzing their contexts of manifestation.

Stimulating the imitation of natural situations, provoking the students' imagination, using games that work on the development of rhythm, improvising the use of diverse materials so that the student himself develops his own rhythm, even the body itself can be used, such as the snapping of fingers and other parts of the body, proposing to the students the assembly of a choreography, or transforming a choreography of a sung toy are some of the possibilities of working in a procedural dimension in the EJA.

In the attitudinal dimension, the dance content can be developed according to Darido and Rangel (2005, p.211) as follows:

- Develop non-discriminatory attitudes towards ability, gender or other reasons for exclusion during the development of a choreography.
- To value and appreciate popular dances as a form of leisure, social integration and part of the community's cultural heritage. To study their origins, to verify the similarities and differences in which the same dangas are presented in different regions and to lead the student to realize that these similarities and differences may be related to the context of each region.
- It is interesting to use the strategy of problematization and the use of films and documentaries that can better illustrate conflicting situations for discussion.
- Emphasize school dance as a non-competitive activity that aims to prepare the student to exercise full citizenship, encouraging them to dance according to their possibilities, i.e. there will be respect for their own and others' physical abilities and capacities; therefore, the demands will take into account individual physical conditions. In this case, inclusion is encouraged, but if dance is approached from a competitive point of view, it could lead to exclusion.

As well as knowing how to do and how to do things, the question of knowing how to be and how to live together in dance work is relevant. The teacher in EJA Physical Education classes must pay attention to the question of discrimination, especially on the part of men, the question of religion which directly interferes with bodily expressions, where there are many misconceptions and polemics surrounding this subject, valuing not only the students who are able to execute the movements with precision, but also those who have managed, within their limitations, to present satisfactory results in terms of their performance. The practice of dance in school is relevant, as long as it doesn't reward the most skillful and exclude those who have a certain difficulty with bodily expression. Bringing back traditional forms of expression is one way of starting a dance project, or one of many possibilities.

3.5 - The pedagogical practice of Wrestling in EJA Physical Education classes.

The first recorded written mention of wrestling dates back to the

Sumerian era, around 4,000 BC, where in the "Poem of Gilgamesh", a king describes a fight in detail. Later, in ancient Egypt, in the tombs of the 5ª Dynasty 2,470 BC, many drawings of wrestling appear where the models were sometimes children, which guarantees the sporting and didactic component of the activity (LEITAO apud MILLER, 2006).

Wrestling, due to its historical history, is somewhat associated with the issue of violence, due to the wars that have taken place throughout the development of civilizations. Perhaps this is one of the reasons for the great resistance to its applicability in the school setting, since practicing this sport would be stimulating the "aggressiveness" of the practitioner, in this case, the student.

According to Darido and Rangel (2005, p. 244) in relation to wrestling at school:

> Among the subjects that can be introduced in school physical education, wrestling is one of those that may encounter the most resistance, usually due to arguments such as lack of space, lack of materials, lack of suitable clothing and, above all, the association with issues of violence.

Finding ways to present wrestling as a theme of body culture is a challenging task for the Physical Education teacher in the search for a new meaning for its applicability within the school.

This task becomes more delicate in the EJA, as some students already have an idea of the purpose of fighting, and tend to resist a new way of looking at a particular subject.

According to Brasil (2002, p.210) the struggles are:

> Disputes in which the opponent must be subdued with techniques and strategies of imbalance, contusion, immobilization or exclusion from a certain space in the combination of defense and attack actions. They are characterized by specific regulations in order to punish attitudes of unnecessary violence and disloyalty. Examples of fights range from tug-of-

> war and arm-wrestling to more complex practices such as capoeira, judo and karate.

It should be noted that body contact is one of the main characteristics of this subject, where the use of a certain movement defines a confrontational situation, with appropriate regulations to prevent disloyalty during the dispute.

There are all kinds of fights around the world these days. It is undeniable that the majority of fights are of Eastern origin, but some of them have emerged in the West. In the West, wrestling is linked solely to the system of fighting and self-defense, unlike the East, which has a philosophical system based on beliefs and religions that prepare the practitioner physically and spiritually (WIKIPEDIA ENCYCLOPEDIA apud MILLER, 2006).

According to Wikipedia apud Miller (2006, p.25) these are types of fights:

- Western: ArtDO, Boxing, Capoeira, Fencing, Full contact, Kombato, Krav Maga, Greco-Roman wrestling, Savate, Wrestling, Vale-Tudo.
- Oriental: Karate, Judo, Taekwondo, Judo, Kung Fu, Muay Thai, Jiu-Jitsu, Sumo, Kempo, Tai Chi Chuan, Aikido, Ninjitsu

The above-mentioned fights that are most popular and have a large number of practitioners in Brazil are Capoeira, Judo and Karate. These disciplines are included in the curriculum of schools and even in Faculties of Physical Education as academic subjects. For this reason, their applicability in EJA Physical Education classes is relevant.

Darido and Rangel (2005, p.249) point out that:

> Wrestling has always been present in human history and is identified by attitudes linked to attack and defense techniques, with the aim of self-protection or military action. In its development, values have been attached to its context, sometimes coming from religions (Buddhism, Taoism,

Shintoism, etc.), sometimes from the sports and Olympic movement.

However, it should be noted that this subject has been little explored in school physical education classes, both in terms of applicability and in terms of selection criteria and specific learning. Presenting wrestling from a conceptual, procedural and attitudinal perspective is necessary in order to give it a new meaning within the school environment.

In a conceptual sense, Darido and Rangel (2006, p. 250) state that:

> We can study fights of Japanese origin, including Judo, Karate, Aikido and Kendo, Chinese fights, such as Tai Chi Chuan, Wu-Shu (Kung Fu), and its offshoots in the East, Tae Kwon Do, Hapkido, and Quaw Ki Do, Western fights, such as Boxing, Kickboxing, Savate, Olympic Wrestling and Brazilian fights, Capoeira and Brazilian Jiu-Jitsu.

Within this context, the following aspects can also be included: the transformations of wrestling, as well as its historical-cultural context and philosophy, the necessary transformations of wrestling to the sports context and also to the school context, recognizing and discussing the influence of the media on the social imagination.

From a procedural point of view, Darido and Rangel (2006, p.250) say that **various types of balance and imbalance can be practiced, as well as some blows that are considered the main ones in the best-known fights, falls and rolls.**

Therefore, proposing variations of manipulative motor skills such as pushing and pulling, stability motor skills such as balance, will be important for the student's knowledge. Another possibility is to alternate opponents, pitting the strongest against the weakest, men against women, the oldest against the youngest, bearing in mind that age differences are common in the EJA, with the aim of showing the differences that exist in each individual and that this diversity must be respected.

In an attitudinal sense, Darido and Rangel (2006, p. 250) expect that:

> There should be active intervention by teachers to re-signify the role of wrestling in the educational context, valuing attitudes of non-violence, respect for colleagues, solving problems through dialogue, the search for justice and solidarity.

Understanding the act of fighting, why to fight, who to fight with, who to fight or what to fight against should be questioned during school physical education lessons, as well as the influence of the media on the appreciation of fighting. Reflecting on these issues is essential for building a critical and active individual in their social context.

3.6 - The pedagogical practice of Gymnastics in Physical Education classes in the EJA.

The modern term gymnastics has a different purpose from the ways in which physical activity has been applied over time. Man's main concern in prehistoric times was to stay alive. During this period, physical exercise took on a utilitarian character, but it did not cease to be part of festivities where the gods were revered (DARIDO and RANGEL, 2005).

Gymnastics has always been related to man's evolutionary process. In each period, its practice, always associated with physical exercise, had a different meaning or objective according to the purposes of each people or nation. Its characteristics and manifestations range from body education, physiological, therapeutic, aesthetic, moral efficacy, military preparation, and the strengthening of body and spirit.

Therefore, Brasil (2002, p. 210) defines the concept of gymnastics as:

> These are bodywork techniques that, in general, take on an individualized character with different purposes. For example, they can be done as preparation for other disciplines, as relaxation, to maintain or recover health, or as a form of recreation, competition and social interaction. They

> sometimes involve the use of materials and equipment and can take place indoors, outdoors or in the water. It should be emphasized that these are contents that have a privileged relationship with the "Knowledge about the body" block, because in gymnastics activities they are made very clear.

As a result, this subject is very rich in terms of learning, leading the individual to get to know their body through activities that require basic movements such as running, jumping, skipping, rolling, among others, which have accompanied the evolutionary process since the dawn of time, and also to understand why certain movements are performed for different purposes.

In the school environment, the practice of gymnastics has always been a conflicting issue. A search in the references on this subject shows that in each period its application had a directed intention, either to maintain the status quo or to form a healthy citizen and defender of the country.

Nowadays, the practice of gymnastics is confused with the issue of sportivization within schools, where its use was only to warm up for some sporting activity, finding a new meaning is relevant for the Physical Education teacher in EJA classes.

Brasil (2002, p.210) points to changes in the ways in which they are applied:

> Nowadays, there are various gymnastics techniques that work in a different way to the traditional ones (rigid, mechanical and repetitive exercises), aiming at the perception of one's own body: being aware of breathing, perceiving the tension and relaxation of muscles, feeling the joints of the spine.

It is up to the teacher to seek out the possibilities of practicing gymnastics and to present it within the school setting. Nowadays, gymnastics is broken down into various objectives: conditioning: acquisition, improvement or enhancement of physical and static conditions, for athletes and non-athletes; therapeutic: prevention and/or treatment of congenital or acquired diseases; alternative: Aims to improve body perception through alternative body practices; Competitive: brings together competitive disciplines; Demonstrative: brings together elements of all gymnastics, and also aims for social interaction; Work: practiced in the workplace (DARIDO and RANGEL, 2005).

Another important aspect for the teacher to consider is working with alternative materials, stimulating the students' creativity, as well as offering a different resource for practicing a certain activity, causing a debate on the issue of working with recyclable material, which directly interferes with human health and the environment.

On a conceptual level, Darido and Rangel (2005, p.233) say that gymnastics can be taught in a way that **allows students to understand the evolution of gymnastics, its history, origin, concept and contexts; students learn to relate the knowledge of gymnastics present in other body culture practices.**

Knowledge of the history of gymnastics provides a clearer understanding of its practice today, its different purposes on the world stage, the role of the media in this area, the power of large companies that profit from products intended for or related to this activity are all issues that teachers should bring to the school stage, seeking to understand how students deal with this issue in the current context.

In relation to the procedural dimension, Darido and Rangel (2005, p.233) propose gymnastics **as a way for students to experience certain elements and learn how to execute gymnastic movements. It includes learning skills and techniques, from the simplest to the most**

elaborate, which are learned according to the characteristics of each student.

The creation of simple and complex choreographic compositions, the preparation and elaboration of gymnastic festivals, the elaboration of physical activity programs are all options that teachers can present to their students during physical education classes at school.

With regard to gymnastics, Darido and Rangel (2005, p. 233) expect students to:

> They tend to develop attitudes, values and norms related to the way students or groups behave. It enables students to respect and value the bodily expressions present in gymnastics and to learn to assume certain behaviors in gymnastics: cooperation, participation, respect for differences, the limits of others and their own, which can be manifested in any other content.

Combating the issue of sexism in the practice of gymnastics is important, given that some body movements are classified as male exercises and others as female. Pointing out the possibilities of each individual in the different activities, respecting their potential for execution, are work alternatives for the Physical Education teacher to emphasize the issue of attitudes in their classes.

3.7 - Assessment in Physical Education in the EJA.

Current curricular proposals, as well as current legislation, give great importance to evaluation, reiterating that it must be continuous, formative and personalized, conceiving it as another element of the teaching-learning process, which allows us to know the results of our didactic support and, consequently, improve them (ZACHARIAS, 2008).

This importance given to evaluation consists of not valuing the quantitative aspect, but showing that the teaching-learning process does not take place through grades and concepts, but in a non-linear and qualitative way.

Learning takes place in a unique way, everyone learns in a different way and at a different time, some more easily, others with more difficulties. Understanding this enables teachers to build a fairer assessment practice. Therefore, a formative approach to assessment is necessary.

According to Zacharias (2008, p.01) on formative evaluation:

> Its aim is not to classify or select. It is based on learning processes, in their cognitive, affective and relational aspects; it is based on meaningful and functional learning that is applied in different contexts and is updated as necessary to keep learning.

When assessment is used to show where progress has been made in the learning process, it becomes an indispensable pedagogical tool in the day-to-day life of the teacher, the school and, above all, the student, who is the subject of learning.

So Zacharias (2008, p.01) points out the characteristics of an evaluation:

> - Assessment should be continuous and integrated into the teacher's diary: this means that it should always be possible in normal situations, avoiding the artificial routine of test situations, in which the student is measured only in that specific situation, abandoning everything that was done in the classroom before the test. The record is of great help to the teacher in carrying out a continuous assessment process.
> - Assessment will be global: when it takes into account the areas of the student's ability: cognitive, motor, interpersonal relations, acting, etc., the student's situation in the various components of the school curriculum.
> - Evaluation will be formative: if it is conceived as a pedagogical means to help the student in their educational process.

Hoffmann *apud* Zacharias (2008, p.01) summarizes:

> Evaluating in this new paradigm is about energizing opportunities for reflective action, accompanied by the teacher, who must enable students to reflect on the world in their learning process, forming critical, liberated beings who participate in the construction of formulated and reformulated truths.

As a result, assessment is a topic that generates a lot of debate and discussion, especially in the field of Physical Education. Because of the influence of sport within the school environment, teacher assessment has been limited to performance, i.e. measuring the fittest and the least fit in the performance of certain motor skills and physical abilities, serving as a strategy for selecting students to compete in school championships.

Darido and Rangel (2005, p.123) comment that:

> Historically, tests of physical sufficiency (at the beginning of the year) and physical efficiency (at the end of the year) were administered in the public school system, formalized in such a way that the teachers' class diaries already contained instructions for carrying them out. These were strength exercises - abdominal, lower limb (kangaroo), upper limb (push-up on the floor, bench and bar) - and general coordination (burpee). According to the number of repetitions, the students were classified into categories: weak, fair, good and excellent.

This type of assessment, whose main characteristic is selectivity, is not acceptable in school, because considering this place to be a democratic space, classifying a group into more able and less able means hindering the social interaction of these individuals. Grading is a punitive assessment tool, which can therefore leave irreversible marks on the student.

In the case of the EJA, where the majority of students are workers, an assessment based on physical performance and with a degree of demand in the execution of motor skills, would lead to a large drop-out rate, given that many of them would not have the courage to do it, especially the females, because of shame and shyness.

A consistent evaluation is structured when the teacher observes who their students are, what their knowledge of certain subjects is, what their facilities and difficulties are in performing a certain movement, and whether at the end of a period the student is able to be critical when the topic studied is addressed.

In an evaluation of the conceptual dimension Darido and Rangel (2005, p.130) say:

> Assessment should consist of observing the use of concepts in teamwork, debates, presentations and, above all, in dialogues between students and between teacher and student. Sometimes there isn't enough time to observe them in all these situations, so you could think about a written test, but you have to be clear about the limitations of actually assessing student learning.

Using the written test as an instrument is relevant, as long as the teacher has the sensitivity to understand what the student wants to get across, and not for them to write down exactly what they have learned without having a critical point of view on the subject covered.

From a procedural point of view, Darido and Rangel (2005, p. 132) argue that:

> We think of assessing motor skills, both basic and specific, as well as physical abilities. However, in this conception it is possible to go further and assess other procedural aspects. For example, it is possible to assess students' ability to collect news stories to which they can add their own personal comments on the journalistic material. The news items can also be organized on panels, on the wall of the classroom or any other space in the school, with themes such as: the importance of physical activity, posture problems and others.

The practical part of Physical Education lessons is interesting as long as it is not assessed in a punitive way, but rather as a way of checking where the difficulty lies and pointing out possible ways of improving. In addition, stimulating the production of work and creativity, such as making magazines or newspapers, contributes to the student's development.

And from an attitudinal point of view, Darido and Rangel (2005, p.130) say that teachers should:

> Knowing what students really value and what their attitudes are should be necessary when conflict situations arise. During learning situations, in games, sports, gymnastics, body knowledge, dances and fights, students are subjected to countless challenges. They have to adapt to new

> movements; to the use of space and material; to certain rules; to expressing feelings, inhibitions and difficulties; in short, variables that make up a very complex teaching and learning environment. Conflicts often break out in these situations.

Conflict is very common among the EJA population, due to students' already formed ideas on certain topics, often influenced by religious issues, family issues, etc. Knowing how to mediate, provoking and opening up a space for debate on a given subject is important so that issues related to attitude are worked on in such a way that everyone can understand their importance and practice them throughout their journey.

In short, the search for a constructive pedagogical practice is a constant challenge for the Physical Education teacher, in any form of Basic Education, but the EJA has a particularity, as it is a course that covers individuals from different age groups, different regions, among other characteristics, which makes the development of teaching a very complex task for the teacher.

Developing work that respects the individuality and diversity of the class is the way forward, based on the conceptual, procedural and attitudinal dimensions. Therefore, the variety of themes that exist within Physical Education becomes a great ally for the teacher in this process of educating, always warning that in the question of evaluation, the student must be analyzed as a whole, in a diagnostic and formative observation, in a qualitative way by the teacher.

FINAL CONSIDERATIONS

It is undeniable that the introduction of Youth and Adult Education in the Brazilian education system has represented a breakthrough in this area. However, it is not enough to bring the individual into the school environment; mechanisms must be put in place to keep them there so that they don't drop out during the training period.

In an attempt to minimize the damage caused by absence from the classroom, mechanisms of function were proposed to guide the teaching-learning process during the construction of the National Curriculum Guidelines for Youth and Adult Education. These functions are classified as: repairing, equalizing and qualifying. Therefore, the aim is to offer an education that makes it possible to recover lost knowledge, respecting the individualities of each student, seeking to know their characteristics and their history becomes a possibility for quality and productive teaching for students in this modality.

In order to investigate whether this modality has suffered any pedagogical influence, two progressive tendencies were analyzed: Liberating pedagogy, whose main idealist is Professor Paulo Freire, considered by many to be the father of Youth and Adult Education. This tendency seeks teaching based on contextualizing the individual's knowledge, in which dialogue becomes the main instrument in this process, and the Critical Social Pedagogy of Content, whose main representative is Professor Jose Carlos Libaneo, This tendency considers the school to be the most democratic space for achieving knowledge, with the teacher as the mediator of this teaching process, where systematized knowledge will be confronted with the knowledge coming from the students, where dialogic practice becomes essential for this event. A characteristic that has become indispensable for education today and which is pointed out all the time in the development of these trends is the practice of dialogue during the teaching-learning process.

Dialogue is an important tool for teachers of Youth and Adult Education, given that this population arrives or returns to the school environment with their minds set on certain issues. Therefore, an attempt to impose a certain fact could cause a great deal of discussion if the teacher assumes the position of "sole" owner of the truth. However, if he opts for dialogic practice, he can start a great debate in which everyone can give their opinion and criticize as participatory subjects.

It is recommended that degree courses focus on the issue of Youth and Adult Education in their curricula, since it is a specific modality with its own peculiarities, a more in-depth and cautious view is necessary.

Being an area of codes and languages, Physical Education in Youth and Adult Education has a relevant function in providing students in this modality with a deeper knowledge of the Corporal Culture of Movement. It's true that its applicability has been gaining ground since the LDB repealed the law that allowed it to be practiced in evening courses (it's important to note that the majority of Youth and Adult Education courses are held in the evening).

Using an approach geared towards the issue of the full citizen, the National Curriculum Parameters are relevant to pedagogical practice in the construction of a meaningful lesson for the Physical Education teacher. Its methodology consists of working with themes from the body culture of movement: sport, games, wrestling, dances and gymnastics, which involve knowledge about the body and rhythmic activity. These themes are presented in three dimensions: conceptual, procedural and attitudinal. Their learning is not restricted to the execution of movement (knowing how to do), but also to the why of movement (knowing how to know) and how to act on movement (knowing how to be and live together).

This pedagogical practice in Youth and Adult Education will be meaningful if we understand that this audience tends to resist the question of what is new, whether out of fear, shame or considering themselves outdated. Beginning to question what they think of the involvement of sport with the media, the search for gyms in the pursuit of the perfect body, and so on, opens up the possibility of productive and relevant work. Teachers need to be aware that their role in the educational process is fundamental to the student's success. In the case of Physical Education classes, an unsuccessful experience during practice can lead to the individual leaving the school environment. Therefore, there is a need for more publications, articles, bibliographies and direct research related to Physical Education and Youth and Adult Education.

It is hoped that this work will contribute to further studies in the field of education and that it will be of great importance in affirming Physical Education as an important curricular component in the Brazilian educational scene.

BIBLIOGRAPHICAL REFERENCES

BARBOSA, L.C.A. **Educapao ffsica escolar e as representapoes sociais.** Rio de Janeiro: Shape, 2001.

BETTI, M. **Educapao Ffsica e sociedade.** Sao Paulo: Movimento, 1991.

BRAZIL. Ministry of Education. Law No. 9.394/96, of December 20, 1996. Establishes the guidelines and bases of education. Brasilia: MEC, p.31-57, 1996.

BRAZIL. Ministry of Education. Secretariat for Primary Education. **Parametros Curriculares Nacionais:** Educapao Fisica/ Secretaria de Educapao Fundamental. Brasilia: MEC, p.114, 1998.

BRAZIL. Ministry of Education. National Education Council. Basic Education Chamber. **National Curriculum Guidelines for youth and adult education**. Basic Education Chamber. Brasilia: MEC, p.68, 2000.

BRAZIL. Ministry of Education. Department of Basic Education. **Curriculum proposal for youth and adult education: second segment of primary education: 5ª to 8ª serie:** Physical Education/ Secretaria de Educapao Fundamental. Brasilia: MEC, p.50, 2002.

BRAZIL. Ministry of Education. Secretariat for Continuing Education, Literacy and Diversity. **Working with youth and adult education: the learning process of students and teachers.** Secretariat for Continuing Education, Literacy and Diversity. Brasilia: MEC, p.50, 2006.

DARIDO, S.C. **Educapao Ffsica na escola: questões e reflexoes.** Rio de

Janeiro: Guanabara Koogan, 2003.

DEMO, P. **Desafios modernos da Educapao.** Petropolis: Vozes, 1999.

FREIRE, Paulo. **Pedagogy of autonomy: knowledge necessary for educational practice.** Sao Paulo: Paz e Terra, 1996.

LIBANEO, J.C. **Democratizapao da escola publica: a pedagogia crftico social dos conteúdos.** Sao Paulo: Loyola, 1985.

MILLER, L.R.S **Wrestling as an educational tool in elementary school.** 2006. 38f. Monograph (Degree in Physical Education) - Faculty of Biological Sciences/Physical Education, UNIG - Rio de Janeiro, 2006.

MIZUKAMI, M.G.N. **Ensino: as abordagens do processo.** Sao Paulo: EPU, 1986.

NISKIER, A. **LDB: a nova lei da educapao.** Rio de Janeiro: Consultor, 1996.

RANGEL, I.C; DARIDO, S.C . **Physical education at school: implications for pedagogical practice.** Rio de Janeiro: Guanabara Koogan, 2005.

ZACHARIAS, V.L.C. **Avaliapao Formativa.** Available at < http:// www.centrorefeducacional.com.br/avaform.htm> accessed on January 23, 2008.

MIX
Papier aus verantwortungsvollen Quellen
Paper from responsible sources
FSC® C105338

Printed by Books on Demand GmbH, Norderstedt / Germany